The Writer's Plotting Workbook

Sample pages:

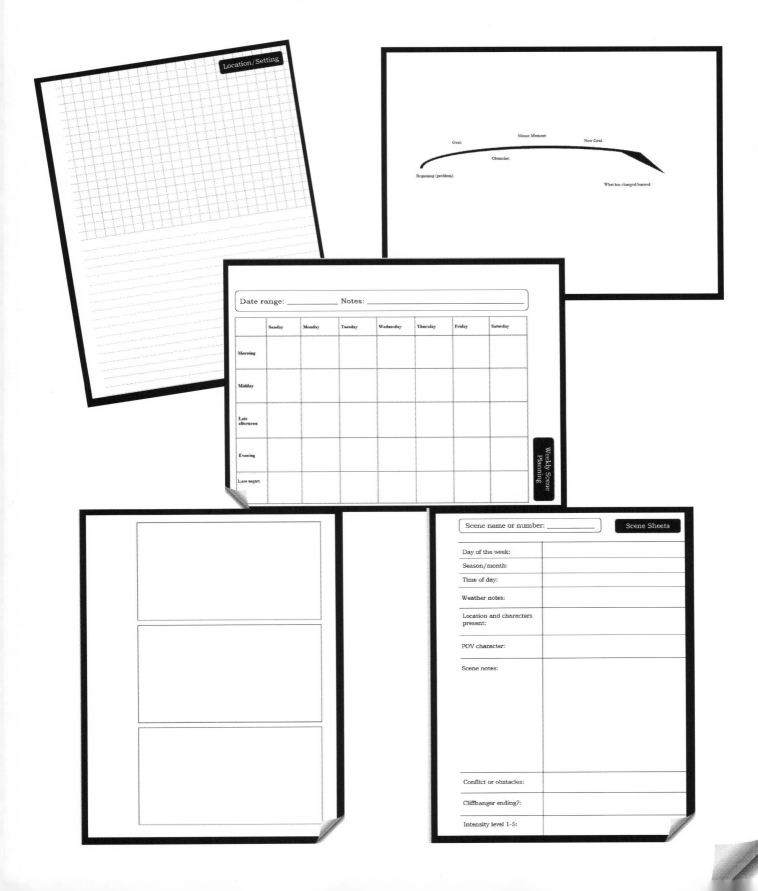

Location/Setting

Goal: Minor Moment: New Goal:

Obstacles:

Beginning (problem):

What has changed/learned:

Date range: _____ Notes: _____

	Sunday	Monday	Tuesday	Wednesday	Thursday	Friday	Saturday
Morning							
Midday							
Late afternoon							
Evening							
Late night							

Weekly Scene Planning

Scene name or number: _____   **Scene Sheets**

Day of the week:	
Season/month:	
Time of day:	
Weather notes:	
Location and characters present:	
POV character:	
Scene notes:	
Conflict or obstacles:	
Cliffhanger ending?:	
Intensity level 1-5:	

Complete plotting: _____

First draft complete: _____

Send to content/developmental editor: _____

Due back from content/
developmental editor: _____

Due to copy editor: _____

Due back from copy editor: _____

Due to proofer: _____

Due to formatter: _____

Due to ARC readers: _____

Complete and formatted: _____

Release date: _____

Working title: _____

G_____

SAMPLE – Skip to the next page for the form

Re_____

Overall book idea – jot down enough to state the main idea	A NAVY SEAL STRUGGLES WITH THE RETURN TO CIVILIAN LIFE UNTIL HE MEETS A WOMAN WHO HELPS HIM ADJUST. HER LIFE IS THREATENED BY PEOPLE FROM HIS PAST.
Hero and Heroine or Protagonist and Antagonist (name and a single sentence about who they are)	LOGAN STONE HERO RECENTLY SEPARATED FROM NAVY SAMANTHA PAGE HEROINE COMPUTER GEEK/HACKER DIYA MOLOV VILLAIN DAUGHTER OF TERRORIST KILLED BY LOGAN AND HIS MEN DURING MILITARY OPERATION
Main conflict – what will your protagonist want and what is in the way?	LOGAN WANTS TO FIND HIS PLACE IN THE WORLD AFTER SERVICE BUT HIS PAST CONTINUES TO HAUNT HIM. WHEN HE HAS TO KILL TO PROTECT SAMANTHA, HIS PTSD IS TRIGGERED AND THERE MAY BE LEGAL CONSEQUENCES FOR HIS ACTIONS.
Primary Trope	PROTECTOR/BODYGUARD
Secondary Trope	REVENGE ALSO A WORKPLACE ROMANCE
Mirror Moment See bit.ly/middleplot	LOGAN TALKS WITH HIS PSYCHIATRIST AND REALIZES IT'S OKAY FOR HIM TO BE HAPPY, REALIZES HE'S HURTING SAMANTHA MORE BY HOLDING HIMSELF BACK FROM HER.
Stakes (physical, psychological, professional)	PHYSICAL THREAT TO SAMANTHA PSYCHOLOGICAL THREAT TO LOGAN

Working title: _____

Genre: _____

Release date: _____

Overall book idea – jot down enough to state the main idea	
Hero and Heroine or Protagonist and Antagonist (name and a single sentence about who they are)	
Main conflict – what will your protagonist want and what is in the way?	
Primary Trope	
Secondary Trope	
Mirror Moment See bit.ly/middleplot	
Stakes (physical, psychological, professional)	

Use the following location sheets to map out cities, towns, floorplans, etc.

Use the top grid portion of the page to sketch maps and the bottom half for notes. You can note which scenes might take place in that location and which characters are connected to the location.

If it's a mystery or thriller, it might be useful to note who has access to the location. You can always change that if you find the need to give someone access based on a plot point.

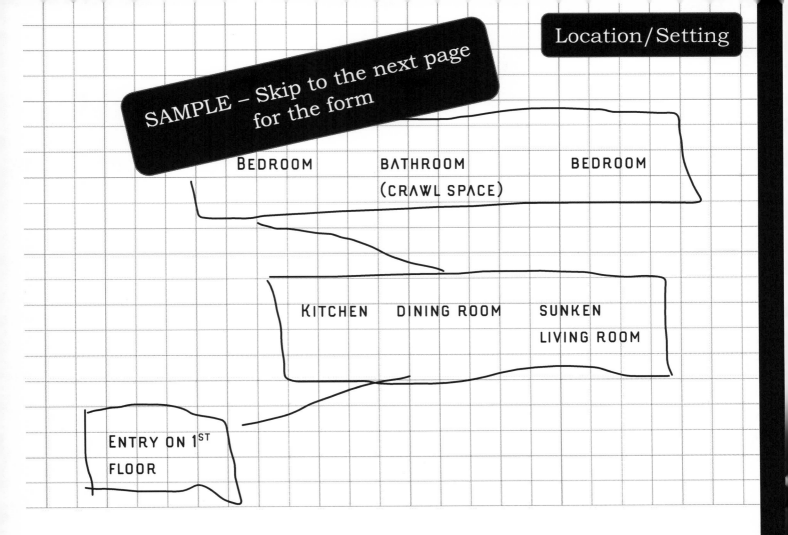

SAMPLE – Skip to the next page for the form

BEDROOM   BATHROOM   BEDROOM
                 (CRAWL SPACE)

KITCHEN   DINING ROOM   SUNKEN
                          LIVING ROOM

ENTRY ON 1ST
FLOOR

AS YOU CAN SEE, MY LOCATION SKETCHES AREN'T DETAILED OR IMPRESSIVE. ONE THE NOTES PAGE, I MIGHT ADD WHERE DOORS ARE OR WHAT THE STYLE OF FURNISHINGS ARE IN EACH ROOM.

FOR THIS BOOK, THIS IS THE LAYOUT OF THE FLOORS IN SAMANTHA'S TOWNHOME. FOR MY NOTES, I WROTE OUT THE LOCATIONS OF THE IMPORTANT INCIDENTS DURING A HOME INVASION WHERE SHE WAS ATTACKED.

LOGAN WAS ABLE TO WARN HER THAT SOMEONE WAS COMING FOR HER. SHE TRIED TO MAKE IT UPSTAIRS TO THE CRAWL SPACE TO BARRICADE HERSELF IN WHILE LOGAN WAS TRYING TO GET TO HER. THE ATTACKERS CAUGHT HER IN THE BATHROOM BEFORE SHE COULD CLOSE THE CRAWL SPACE.

LOGAN KILLED ONE ATTACKER IN THE ENTRYWAY TO THE TOWNHOME ON THE FIRST LEVEL, ANOTHER IN THE HALLWAY OUTSIDE THE BATHROOM, AND THE LAST IN THE BATHROOM.

Use the following sheets to
plan your protagonist,
antagonist, hero, heroine,
villain, or any other
main characters.

Create a story arc for
each character.

Name: LOGAN STONE

Role: HERO

Age: 34

Gender: MALE

Race: CAUCASIAN

Hair and eye color: HAIR ALMOST BLACK. DARK BROWN EYES. 5 O'CLOCK SHADOW

Complexion: TANNED

Build: 6'2" LARGE AND MUSCULAR. BROAD SHOULDERS. INJURY IN LEG, GETS STIFF

Style/appearance: NO BIZ SUITS. SLACKS AND SHIRT FOR WORK. BDUS ON THE WEEKENDS.

Habits/quirks: HYPERVIGILANT. AVOIDS DRIVING IN TRAFFIC. RUBS LEG WHEN STIFF. RUBS BACK OF NECK OFTEN.

Flaw: PTSD

Siblings: NONE

Parents: MOTHER DIED WHEN HE WAS 7. FATHER IS AN ALCOHOLIC.

Family life: AFTER MOTHER'S DEATH HE WAS NEGLECTED BY FATHER. LARGELY LEFT TO RAISE HIMSELF.

Current home: APARTMENT BLACKOUT CURTAINS AND KNIVES/GUNS HIDDEN—TOO MANY TO BE HEALTHY.

Backstory/tragic past: LAST YEAR IN MILITARY WAS IN BLACK OPS. SENT INTO AFTER A TERRORIST BUT INTEL WAS BAD. WIFE AND SONS THERE WHEN OP WENT BAD. ALL KILLED.

Results of backstory/past: SUFFERS PTSD AND DOUBTS HIMSELF AND DECISIONS HE MADE AS LEADER OF THAT OP. ADULT DAUGHTER OF THE TERRORIST SURVIVED AND WANTS REVENGE.

Internal Conflict: GUILT OVER HIS JOB AND SAMANTHA WHEN MANY OF HIS TEAM DIDN'T COME HOME OR HAVE SERIOUS INJURIES THEY'RE DEALING WITH.

WANTS TO BE HAPPY, BUT DOESN'T FEEL LIKE HE DESERVES IT.

External Conflict DIYA IS COMING AFTER HIM AND OTHER MEMBERS OF HER TEAM. DIYA FOCUSES ON SAMANTHA AS A WAY TO HURT LOGAN. WHEN LOGAN KILLS MEN WHO CAME AFTER SAM, HE FACES LEGAL CONSEQUENCES.

SAMPLE

Goal:

CONVERSATION WITH ERNIE ABOUT HIS INSTINCTS AND SAFETY, ABOUT WHAT SAM NEEDS, AND ABOUT WHAT LOGAN DESERVES TO FEEL WITHOUT HAVING TO FEEL GUILTY OVER IT.

STOP DIYA'S ATTACKS AGAINST SAMANTHA. CONTINUE HIS COUNSELING AND PROGRESS WITH PTSD.

Mirror Moment:

New Goal:

Obstacles:

HE'S TRYING TO DEAL WITH PTSD WITHOUT ANY SUPPORT OR COUNSELING.

PEOPLE FROM HIS PAST ARE COMING AFTER SAMANTHA.

What has changed/learned:

HE IS NOT A DANGER TO PEOPLE AROUND HIM. HE ACTED BASED ON YEARS OF TRAINING AND HONED SKILL IN MILITARY WHEN HE KILLED TO PROTECT SAM — THAT DOESN'T MAKE HIM A DANGER TO BE AROUND.

SAM NEEDS HIM AS MUCH AS HE NEEDS HER. IT IS OKAY FOR HIM TO BE HAPPY WITH HER AND TO BUILD A LIFE WITH HER EVEN THOUGH SOME OF HIS MEN CAME HOME WITH INJURIES OR DIDN'T RETURN HOME ALIVE.

INITIALLY, TO SURVIVE DAY-TO-DAY WITH HIS PTSD SYMPTOMS. AS THE STORY PROGRESSES, HIS GOAL IS TO KEEP SAMANTHA SAFE.

Beginning (problem):

LOGAN HAS PTSD AND GUILT OVER BEING HOME SAFE WITH A GOOD JOB WHILE HIS TEAM IS NOT.

Internal Conflict:

External Conflict

Siblings:

Parents:

Family life:

Current home:

Backstory/tragic past:

Results of backstory/past:

Name:

Role:

Age:

Gender:

Race:

Hair and eye color:

Complexion:

Build:

Style/appearance:

Habits/quirks:

Flaw:

What is the character's main goal and motivation/what do they most want:

How does this character hide from the world/what mask do they wear for <u>others</u>:

How will this character grow (or not) during the story/what does this character need to <u>learn</u>:

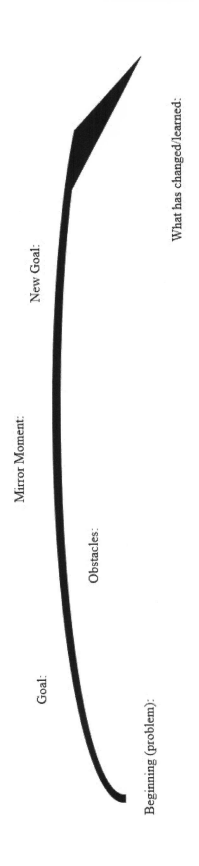

What has changed/learned:

New Goal:

Mirror Moment:

Obstacles:

Goal:

Beginning (problem):

Internal Conflict:

External Conflict

Siblings:

Parents:

Family life:

Current home:

Backstory/tragic past:

Results of backstory/past:

Name:

Role:

Age:

Gender:

Race:

Hair and eye color:

Complexion:

Build:

Style/appearance:

Habits/quirks:

Flaw:

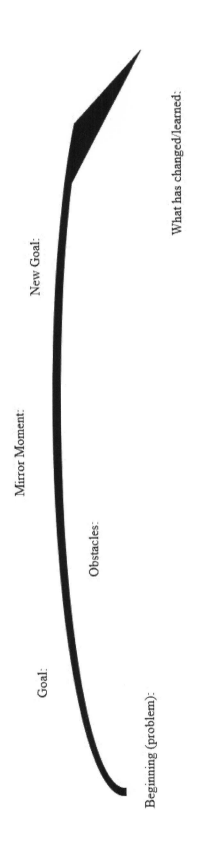

What has changed/learned:

New Goal:

Mirror Moment:

Obstacles:

Goal:

Beginning (problem):

Internal Conflict:

External Conflict

Siblings:

Parents:

Family life:

Current home:

Backstory/tragic past:

Results of backstory/past:

Name:

Role:

Age:

Gender:

Race:

Hair and eye color:

Complexion:

Build:

Style/appearance:

Habits/quirks:

Flaw:

What is the character's main goal and motivation/what do they most want:

How does this character hide from the world/what mask do they wear for <u>others</u>:

How will this character grow (or not) during the story/what does this character need to <u>learn</u>:

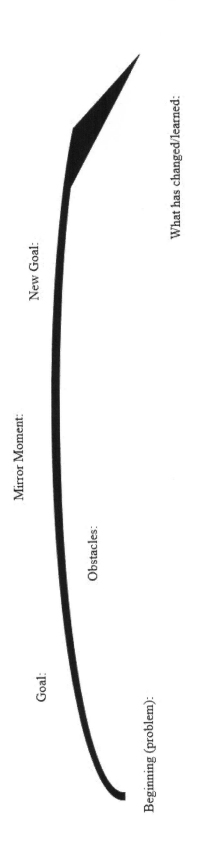

What has changed/learned:

New Goal:

Mirror Moment:

Obstacles:

Goal:

Beginning (problem):

Use the following sheets to plan out your side characters.

In the "Connected to" section, note which main character the side character is related to (whether through family, work, or friendship) and what their role is in the story.

If you're writing a suspense or mystery, this is a good time to start thinking about red herrings and which characters might throw your readers off track.

Name: ERNIE GREEN

Role/purpose: LOGAN'S COUNSELOR — WILL BE CRUCIAL TO LOGAN'S MIRROR MOMENT AND RECOVERY.

Description: AFRICAN AMERICAN IN HIS FORTIES, ROUND FACE, LAID BACK. VETERAN DESERT STORM. DOUBLE AMPUTEE BELOW THE KNEES.

Connected to: LOGAN STONE — COUNSELOR, REFERRED TO HIM BY CHAD THOMPSON.

Notes: LAID BACK AND DOESN'T PUSH. SHARED HISTORY HELPS HIM REACH OTHER VETERANS. WILL BE IMPORTANT TO LOGAN'S DEALING OF TRAUMA AFTER LOGAN HAS TO KILL TO PROTECT SAMANTHA.

Name:

Role/purpose:

Description:

Connected to:

Notes:

Name:

Role/purpose:

Description:

Connected to:

Notes:

Name:

Role/purpose:

Description:

Connected to:

Notes:

Name:

Role/purpose:

Description:

Connected to:

Notes:

Name:

Role/purpose:

Description:

Connected to:

Notes:

Name:

Role/purpose:

Description:

Connected to:

Notes:

Name:

Role/purpose:

Description:

Connected to:

Notes:

Name:

Role/purpose:

Description:

Connected to:

Notes:

Diya Molov

Family was killed by Logan's team. Goes after Sam for revenge.

Yoshi Bogolomov

Cousin to Diya Her right-hand-man

Peter Gatorelli

Black hat hacker PriorOfTheOri — screen name.

Logan Stone

Ernie Green counselor

Eric Westbrook

Assistant district attorney prosecuting Logan

Jack Sutton

Boss Sam and Logan

Chad Thompson

Friend and co-worker Sam and Logan.

Kelly Sutton and Jennie Thompson

Friends Samantha

Samantha Page

BillieBurke — screen name of white hat hacker who took out Lorenzo and others. Sam's online identity

Screen name BillieBurke is a play on Glinda the Good Witch. .

Lorenzo Alonso

Sam helped prove his guilt in human trafficking ring.

On the following Genre Specific Details sheets, take some time to write anything specific to your genre.

If you write in fantasy, write out the rules of the magic in your world or terms specific to your world.

If you write sci-fi, you might add planet names or tech terms for your world to this section.

If you write suspense or mystery, think through how your crime will occur, and make note of red herrings you need to add to your plot. Think through the evidence that might be discovered (or not) through the plot.

If you write romantic suspense, when and how will your heroine end up in trouble? Will she have a hand in her own rescue or be simply a damsel in distress?

For a historical novel, note any details you want to include and any research you need to do.

Now it's time to plot each of the scenes in your book.

The scenes you need will depend largely on the type of book you are writing, but here is a loose guide to the scenes I plot out with a romantic suspense. These elements come from a mashup of numerous plotting courses, books, and sources. I'm sure you'll recognize a lot of it.

- Intro the hero and heroine (or if this isn't a romance, show your protagonist). Show their current life and what's missing from it, whether they realize something is missing or not. I try to include something here that either makes the reader want to root for the character or makes the reader feel for the character, even if they aren't all that likeable yet.
- I like to get an element of mystery or action/adventure right in the beginning. A crime, a hint at some intrigue, the initiating event that sets the character on the path of the adventure.
- In the case of a romance, I'll put the meet cute in by chapter three, if not earlier.
- I'll show the reader what's at stake. Is it a threat to a character or the city/town? Something emotional? The character's career? Making the reader care is crucial, so that's always on my list.
- Early on, I'll have the "no way" moment where the hero and heroine think "no way" can I have a relationship/find love/be with this person.
- On the suspense side of the plot, I start to crank up the pressure, either by adding a ticking time bomb, turning a friend into a foe, or increasing the danger in some way. Sometimes I'll have the villain's POV sprinkled into the book. Sometimes, I don't.
- If I haven't done it sooner, it's time to add the adhesion plot point. What is going to push my hero and heroine together and keep them together?
- One step forward for my good guys. A clue in the mystery, some hope that they might save the world, some step toward the ultimate goal.
- A "no way" moment number two for my hero and heroine, or maybe they decide "yes, but only in a purely physical, so-strings-attached way."
- Two steps back for the good guys. A lead didn't pan out, someone is hurt, the timeline is moved up.
- Friendship starting between hero and heroine? Or maybe an inkling that the heat they've been feeling could go somewhere.
- I'll usually put something from the bad guy's POV here to show they've had a set back. Or if this isn't a book where the villain has a POV, then there will be a scene where the police see evidence the bad guy is unravelling, thins aren't going as planned for him or her.
- Deepening desire between my hero and heroine. Maybe this could work. Maybe it's worth the risk. Let's try this.
- The bad guy strikes back, tries to solve the problem he has or increases threat in some way.
- Meanwhile, as my hero and heroine are trying to resolve the mystery or hunt the baddie, they have to develop true feelings for each other. This can be a tough balance. You need to show they're open to the possibility of love. At the halfway mark, your hero or heroine (or both) needs a mirror moment. Read up on mirror moments from James Scott Bell for more on this.

Use the following sheets to plan your scenes

There are week, month, and yearly calendars for planning.

These are followed by index card sheets for story-boarding and scene planning sheets for detailed mapping of each scene.

Pay careful attention to conflict and intensity level to be sure you vary the intensity of your scenes.

SAMPLE – Skip to the next page for the form

Date range: ENTER THE DATES OR
GENERAL SEASON

Notes: COVERS FIRST TWO CHAPTERS — THEN TIME JUMPS TWO WEEKS FORWARD

Dates range:	Sunday	Monday	Tuesday	Wednesday	Thursday	Friday	Saturday
Morning		LOGAN AND SAM MEET AT WORK.					
Midday		LOGAN AND SAM LUNCH — SHE RECOGNIZES HIS PTSD SYMPTOMS					
Late afternoon							
Evening					COMPANY PARTY LOGAN GETS NEWS ON DIYA AND SAM LIP READS		
Late night							

Date range: _____

Notes: _____

	Sunday	Monday	Tuesday	Wednesday	Thursday	Friday	Saturday
Morning							
Midday							
Late afternoon							
Evening							
Late night:							

Weekly Scene Planning

Date range: _____

Notes: _____

	Sunday	Monday	Tuesday	Wednesday	Thursday	Friday	Saturday
Morning							
Midday							
Late afternoon							
Evening							
Late night:							

Date range: _____

Notes: _____

	Sunday	Monday	Tuesday	Wednesday	Thursday	Friday	Saturday
Morning							
Midday							
Late afternoon							
Evening							
Late night:							

Date range: _____

Notes: _____

	Sunday	Monday	Tuesday	Wednesday	Thursday	Friday	Saturday
Morning							
Midday							
Late afternoon							
Evening							
Late night:							

Weekly Scene Planning

Date range: _____

Notes: _____

	Sunday	Monday	Tuesday	Wednesday	Thursday	Friday	Saturday
Morning							
Midday							
Late afternoon							
Evening							
Late night:							

Date range: _____

Notes: _____

Sunday	Monday	Tuesday	Wednesday	Thursday	Friday	Saturday

Monthly Scene
Planning

Date range: _____

Notes: _____

Sunday	Monday	Tuesday	Wednesday	Thursday	Friday	Saturday

Date range: _____ _____

Notes: _____ _____

Sunday	Monday	Tuesday	Wednesday	Thursday	Friday	Saturday

Date range: _____

Notes: _____

Sunday	Monday	Tuesday	Wednesday	Thursday	Friday	Saturday

January

Sunday	Monday	Tuesday	Wednesday	Thursday	Friday	Saturday

February

Sunday	Monday	Tuesday	Wednesday	Thursday	Friday	Saturday

March

Sunday	Monday	Tuesday	Wednesday	Thursday	Friday	Saturday

April

Sunday	Monday	Tuesday	Wednesday	Thursday	Friday	Saturday

May

Sunday	Monday	Tuesday	Wednesday	Thursday	Friday	Saturday

June

Sunday	Monday	Tuesday	Wednesday	Thursday	Friday	Saturday

July

Sunday	Monday	Tuesday	Wednesday	Thursday	Friday	Saturday

August

Sunday	Monday	Tuesday	Wednesday	Thursday	Friday	Saturday

September

Sunday	Monday	Tuesday	Wednesday	Thursday	Friday	Saturday

October

Sunday	Monday	Tuesday	Wednesday	Thursday	Friday	Saturday

November

Sunday	Monday	Tuesday	Wednesday	Thursday	Friday	Saturday

December

Sunday	Monday	Tuesday	Wednesday	Thursday	Friday	Saturday

SAMPLE – Skip to the next page for the form

SCENE ONE (SOME AUTHORS NUMBER AND SOME USE NAMES — YOU COULD NAME THIS MEET CUTE SCENE

LOGAN POV - LOGAN IS IN OFFICE EARLY — CHAT WITH JACK, ESTABLISH PTSD IS CAUSING NEED TO ARRIVE EARLY. THEY OVER HEAR SAMANTHA AND JENNIE TALKING.

SWITCH TO SAM POV — SHE COMPLAINS TO JENNIE THAT THE NEW TECH TEAM COMING IN IS ALL SUPER HOT GUYS — WHY CAN'T JACK HIRE SOME NORMAL LOOKING PEOPLE LIKE HER AND THE REST OF THE WORLD INSTEAD OF TOTAL HOTTIES? IT'S BAD ENOUGH JACK IS SEX-ON-A-STICK BUT WHY DOES HE HAVE TO HIRE A TEAM THAT LOOKS LIKE THIS?

JACK AND LOGAN OVERHEAR AND SHE IS INTRODUCED TO LOGAN BY A LAUGHING JACK. HER FIRST WORD TO LOGAN IS "GAH."

Scene name or number: MEET CUTE	Scene sheets

Day of the week:	MONDAY
Season/month:	
Time of day:	MORNING
Weather notes:	NOT MENTIONED IN THE SCENE
Location and characters present:	SUTTON CAPITAL OFFICES — TOWARD THE BACK WHERE LOGAN'S OFFICE IS
POV character:	BEGIN AS LOGAN AND SWITCH TO SAMANTHA
Scene notes:	LOGAN POV - LOGAN IS IN OFFICE EARLY — CHAT WITH JACK, ESTABLISH PTSD IS CAUSING NEED TO ARRIVE EARLY. THEY OVER HEAR SAMANTHA AND JENNIE TALKING. SWITCH TO SAM POV — SHE TELLS JENNIE IT SUCKS THAT THE NEW TECH TEAM COMING IN IS ALL SUPER HOT GUYS — WHY CAN'T JACK HIRE SOME NORMAL LOOKING PEOPLE LIKE HER AND THE REST OF THE WORLD INSTEAD OF TOTAL HOTTIES. IT'S BAD ENOUGH JACK IS SEX-ON-A-STICK BUT WHY DOES HE HAVE TO HIRE A TEAM THAT LOOKS LIKE THEM. JACK AND LOGAN OVERHEAR AND SHE IS INTRODUCED TO LOGAN BY A LAUGHING JACK. HER FIRST WORD TO LOGAN IS "GAH."
Conflict or obstacles:	LOGAN TRYING TO COVER HIS PTSD FROM OTHERS. SAMANTHA TRYING NOT TO EMBARRASS HERSELF.
Cliffhanger ending?:	NO, BUT ENDS WITH HUMOR.
Intensity level 1-5:	2

Day of the week:

Season/month:

Time of day:

Weather notes:

Location and characters present:

POV character:

Scene notes:

Conflict or obstacles:

Cliffhanger ending?:

Intensity level 1-5:

Scene name or number: _____

Day of the week:	
Season/month:	
Time of day:	
Weather notes:	
Location and characters present:	
POV character:	
Scene notes:	
Conflict or obstacles:	
Cliffhanger ending?:	
Intensity level 1-5:	

Scene name or number: _____

Day of the week:

Season/month:

Time of day:

Weather notes:

Location and characters present:

POV character:

Scene notes:

Conflict or obstacles:

Cliffhanger ending?:

Intensity level 1-5:

Scene name or number: _____

Day of the week:	
Season/month:	
Time of day:	
Weather notes:	
Location and characters present:	
POV character:	
Scene notes:	
Conflict or obstacles:	
Cliffhanger ending?:	
Intensity level 1-5:	

Scene name or number: _____

Day of the week:	
Season/month:	
Time of day:	
Weather notes:	
Location and characters present:	
POV character:	
Scene notes:	
Conflict or obstacles:	
Cliffhanger ending?:	
Intensity level 1-5:	

Scene name or number: _____

Day of the week:

Season/month:

Time of day:

Weather notes:

Location and characters present:

POV character:

Scene notes:

Conflict or obstacles:

Cliffhanger ending?:

Intensity level 1-5:

Scene name or number: _____

Day of the week:

Season/month:

Time of day:

Weather notes:

Location and characters present:

POV character:

Scene notes:

Conflict or obstacles:

Cliffhanger ending?:

Intensity level 1-5:

Scene name or number: _____

Day of the week:	
Season/month:	
Time of day:	
Weather notes:	
Location and characters present:	
POV character:	
Scene notes:	
Conflict or obstacles:	
Cliffhanger ending?:	
Intensity level 1-5:	

Scene name or number: _____

Day of the week:

Season/month:

Time of day:

Weather notes:

Location and characters present:

POV character:

Scene notes:

Conflict or obstacles:

Cliffhanger ending?:

Intensity level 1-5:

Scene name or number: _____

Day of the week:

Season/month:

Time of day:

Weather notes:

Location and characters present:

POV character:

Scene notes:

Conflict or obstacles:

Cliffhanger ending?:

Intensity level 1-5:

Day of the week:

Season/month:

Time of day:

Weather notes:

Location and characters present:

POV character:

Scene notes:

Conflict or obstacles:

Cliffhanger ending?:

Intensity level 1-5:

Scene name or number: _____

Day of the week:

Season/month:

Time of day:

Weather notes:

Location and characters present:

POV character:

Scene notes:

Conflict or obstacles:

Cliffhanger ending?:

Intensity level 1-5:

Scene name or number: _____

Day of the week:

Season/month:

Time of day:

Weather notes:

Location and characters present:

POV character:

Scene notes:

Conflict or obstacles:

Cliffhanger ending?:

Intensity level 1-5:

Scene name or number: _____

Day of the week:

Season/month:

Time of day:

Weather notes:

Location and characters present:

POV character:

Scene notes:

Conflict or obstacles:

Cliffhanger ending?:

Intensity level 1-5:

Scene name or number: _____

Day of the week:	
Season/month:	
Time of day:	
Weather notes:	
Location and characters present:	
POV character:	
Scene notes:	
Conflict or obstacles:	
Cliffhanger ending?:	
Intensity level 1-5:	

Scene name or number: _____

Day of the week:	
Season/month:	
Time of day:	
Weather notes:	
Location and characters present:	
POV character:	
Scene notes:	
Conflict or obstacles:	
Cliffhanger ending?:	
Intensity level 1-5:	

Scene name or number: _____

Day of the week:	
Season/month:	
Time of day:	
Weather notes:	
Location and characters present:	
POV character:	
Scene notes:	
Conflict or obstacles:	
Cliffhanger ending?:	
Intensity level 1-5:	

Scene name or number: _____

Day of the week:	
Season/month:	
Time of day:	
Weather notes:	
Location and characters present:	
POV character:	
Scene notes:	
Conflict or obstacles:	
Cliffhanger ending?:	
Intensity level 1-5:	

Scene name or number: _____

Day of the week:	
Season/month:	
Time of day:	
Weather notes:	
Location and characters present:	
POV character:	
Scene notes:	
Conflict or obstacles:	
Cliffhanger ending?:	
Intensity level 1-5:	

Day of the week:

Season/month:

Time of day:

Weather notes:

Location and characters present:

POV character:

Scene notes:

Conflict or obstacles:

Cliffhanger ending?:

Intensity level 1-5:

Scene name or number: _____

Day of the week:	
Season/month:	
Time of day:	
Weather notes:	
Location and characters present:	
POV character:	
Scene notes:	
Conflict or obstacles:	
Cliffhanger ending?:	
Intensity level 1-5:	

Scene name or number: _____

Day of the week:	
Season/month:	
Time of day:	
Weather notes:	
Location and characters present:	
POV character:	
Scene notes:	
Conflict or obstacles:	
Cliffhanger ending?:	
Intensity level 1-5:	

Scene name or number: _____

Day of the week:	
Season/month:	
Time of day:	
Weather notes:	
Location and characters present:	
POV character:	
Scene notes:	
Conflict or obstacles:	
Cliffhanger ending?:	
Intensity level 1-5:	

Day of the week:	
Season/month:	
Time of day:	
Weather notes:	
Location and characters present:	
POV character:	
Scene notes:	
Conflict or obstacles:	
Cliffhanger ending?:	
Intensity level 1-5:	

Scene name or number: _____

Day of the week:	
Season/month:	
Time of day:	
Weather notes:	
Location and characters present:	
POV character:	
Scene notes:	
Conflict or obstacles:	
Cliffhanger ending?:	
Intensity level 1-5:	

Scene name or number: _____

Day of the week:	
Season/month:	
Time of day:	
Weather notes:	
Location and characters present:	
POV character:	
Scene notes:	
Conflict or obstacles:	
Cliffhanger ending?:	
Intensity level 1-5:	

Scene name or number: _____

Day of the week:	
Season/month:	
Time of day:	
Weather notes:	
Location and characters present:	
POV character:	
Scene notes:	
Conflict or obstacles:	
Cliffhanger ending?:	
Intensity level 1-5:	

Scene name or number: _____

Day of the week:	
Season/month:	
Time of day:	
Weather notes:	
Location and characters present:	
POV character:	
Scene notes:	
Conflict or obstacles:	
Cliffhanger ending?:	
Intensity level 1-5:	

Scene name or number: _____

Day of the week:	
Season/month:	
Time of day:	
Weather notes:	
Location and characters present:	
POV character:	
Scene notes:	
Conflict or obstacles:	
Cliffhanger ending?:	
Intensity level 1-5:	

Scene name or number: _____

Day of the week:

Season/month:

Time of day:

Weather notes:

Location and characters present:

POV character:

Scene notes:

Conflict or obstacles:

Cliffhanger ending?:

Intensity level 1-5:

Scene name or number: _____

Day of the week:

Season/month:

Time of day:

Weather notes:

Location and characters present:

POV character:

Scene notes:

Conflict or obstacles:

Cliffhanger ending?:

Intensity level 1-5:

Scene name or number: _____

Day of the week:	
Season/month:	
Time of day:	
Weather notes:	
Location and characters present:	
POV character:	
Scene notes:	
Conflict or obstacles:	
Cliffhanger ending?:	
Intensity level 1-5:	

Scene name or number: _____

Day of the week:	
Season/month:	
Time of day:	
Weather notes:	
Location and characters present:	
POV character:	
Scene notes:	
Conflict or obstacles:	
Cliffhanger ending?:	
Intensity level 1-5:	

Scene name or number: _____

Day of the week:

Season/month:

Time of day:

Weather notes:

Location and characters present:

POV character:

Scene notes:

Conflict or obstacles:

Cliffhanger ending?:

Intensity level 1-5:

Scene name or number: _____

Day of the week:	
Season/month:	
Time of day:	
Weather notes:	
Location and characters present:	
POV character:	
Scene notes:	
Conflict or obstacles:	
Cliffhanger ending?:	
Intensity level 1-5:	

Scene name or number: _____

Day of the week:	
Season/month:	
Time of day:	
Weather notes:	
Location and characters present:	
POV character:	
Scene notes:	
Conflict or obstacles:	
Cliffhanger ending?:	
Intensity level 1-5:	

Scene name or number: _____

Day of the week:	
Season/month:	
Time of day:	
Weather notes:	
Location and characters present:	
POV character:	
Scene notes:	
Conflict or obstacles:	
Cliffhanger ending?:	
Intensity level 1-5:	

Day of the week:

Season/month:

Time of day:

Weather notes:

Location and characters present:

POV character:

Scene notes:

Conflict or obstacles:

Cliffhanger ending?:

Intensity level 1-5:

Scene name or number: _____

Day of the week:	
Season/month:	
Time of day:	
Weather notes:	
Location and characters present:	
POV character:	
Scene notes:	
Conflict or obstacles:	
Cliffhanger ending?:	
Intensity level 1-5:	

Scene name or number: _____

Day of the week:	
Season/month:	
Time of day:	
Weather notes:	
Location and characters present:	
POV character:	
Scene notes:	
Conflict or obstacles:	
Cliffhanger ending?:	
Intensity level 1-5:	

Scene name or number: _____

Day of the week:

Season/month:

Time of day:

Weather notes:

Location and characters present:

POV character:

Scene notes:

Conflict or obstacles:

Cliffhanger ending?:

Intensity level 1-5:

Scene name or number: _____

Day of the week:

Season/month:

Time of day:

Weather notes:

Location and characters present:

POV character:

Scene notes:

Conflict or obstacles:

Cliffhanger ending?:

Intensity level 1-5:

Scene name or number: _____

Day of the week:	
Season/month:	
Time of day:	
Weather notes:	
Location and characters present:	
POV character:	
Scene notes:	
Conflict or obstacles:	
Cliffhanger ending?:	
Intensity level 1-5:	

Scene name or number: _____

Day of the week:	
Season/month:	
Time of day:	
Weather notes:	
Location and characters present:	
POV character:	
Scene notes:	
Conflict or obstacles:	
Cliffhanger ending?:	
Intensity level 1-5:	

Scene name or number: _____

Day of the week:

Season/month:

Time of day:

Weather notes:

Location and characters present:

POV character:

Scene notes:

Conflict or obstacles:

Cliffhanger ending?:

Intensity level 1-5:

Scene name or number: _____

Day of the week:	
Season/month:	
Time of day:	
Weather notes:	
Location and characters present:	
POV character:	
Scene notes:	
Conflict or obstacles:	
Cliffhanger ending?:	
Intensity level 1-5:	

Scene name or number: _____

Day of the week:	
Season/month:	
Time of day:	
Weather notes:	
Location and characters present:	
POV character:	
Scene notes:	
Conflict or obstacles:	
Cliffhanger ending?:	
Intensity level 1-5:	